Sweet Autumn

COLOR BY NUMBER FOR ADULTS

By Aunty Kelthy

"Revel in life's vibrant tapestry!"

Copyright © 2023 by Aunty Kelthy

A LITTLE INSPIRATION FROM THE AUTHOR

Hey, welcome to Aunt Kelthy's bookstore!

I'm an elderly woman who, like many retirees, was struggling with feelings of boredom and a lack of purpose. But I knew that entertainment was important even as I aged, and so I decided to channel my creativity into creating something that would bring

I've always loved art and books, and I have a passion for gardening.
So, I decided to combine these interests and create coloring books

For me, the process of creating these coloring books has been therapeutic. It's given me a sense of purpose and satisfaction that I didn't know I was missing. And, I'm grateful for the opportunity to share my love of art with others and bring a little bit of joy into their lives as well.

I know that entertainment is essential, especially as we age, and that's why I've dedicated myself to creating these coloring books. They're not just a pastime; they're a source of inspiration, a way to relax, and a reminder that no matter

It's been an incredible journey so far, and I'm grateful for every person who has picked up one of my coloring books and found joy in it. I hope that my creations continue to inspire and bring happiness to people all around the world.

Thank you so much for purchasing this Sweet Autumn Color By Number!
Your support allows me to create many great books.

COLOR BY NUMBER
Coloring made fun and easy!

RELAX AND HAVE FUN
Let your worries slip away as you immerse yourself in coloring these beautiful images. Feel free to color while listening to your favorite music, watching TV, or simply lounging in bed - do whatever relaxes you the most! You can even take the coloring book with you anywhere you go, whether it's on the train or at a cafe. Coloring is therapeutic and an excellent way to relieve stress and promote relaxation.

CHOOSE YOUR COLORING TOOLS
Everyone has their preferred coloring tools, whether it's markers, crayons, colored pencils, or even paints! Don't hesitate to use whichever tool you like best. However, if you decide to use markers or paints, it's a good idea to place a blank sheet of paper or cardboard behind each image to prevent colors from bleeding onto the next page.

TEST OUT YOUR COLORS
Feel free to experiment with colors on our Color Chart located at the back of the book. You can utilize "Your Color Palette" to create your own unique color combinations, then cut this page out to compare each time you color. This way, you can ensure the colors match your preferences.

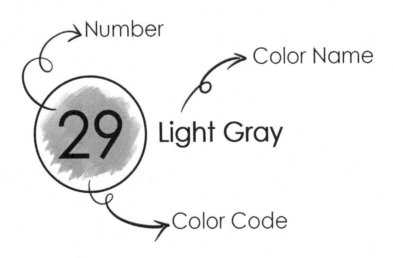

Number

Color Name

29 Light Gray

Color Code

Relax and Enjoy!

YOUR COLOR PALETTE

1 Orange Red	11 Light Yellow	21 Dark Purple
2 Dark Orange	12 Light Green	22 Medium Purple
3 Dark Brown	13 Medium Green	23 Pink
4 Light Orange	14 Dark Green	24 Dark Red
5 Medium Brown	15 Cyan	25 Medium Red
6 Light Brown	16 Light Blue	26 Black
7 Medium Orange	17 Medium Blue	27 Dark Gray
8 Yellow Orange	18 Dark Blue	28 Medium Gray
9 Dark Yellow	19 Blue Purple	29 Light Gray
10 Medium Yellow	20 Light Purple	30 White

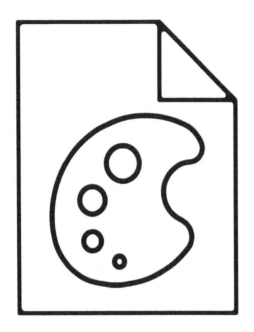

This palette
belongs to this book

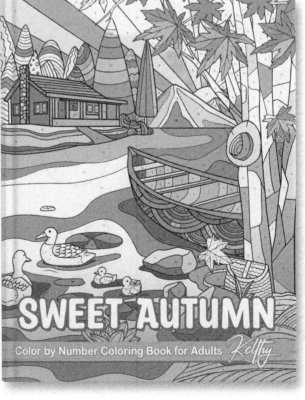

THIS BOOK
BELONGS TO

Write down your favorite aspects of this book:

....

....

....

....

....

....

....

....

....

....

....

....

....

....

Copyright © 2023 by Aunty Kelthy

Thank you for trusting us by purchasing our books.

Your trust in us means a lot, and we truly hope that you will find joy and satisfaction in coloring our unique designs.

If our book meets your expectations, we kindly request you to consider leaving a positive review, as it inspires us to strive for even greater excellence in

Once again, thank you for your support and we hope that our coloring book will bring a little bit of creativity and

Made in the USA
Coppell, TX
16 September 2023

21633358R00033